THE
SEMINOLE
INDIANS

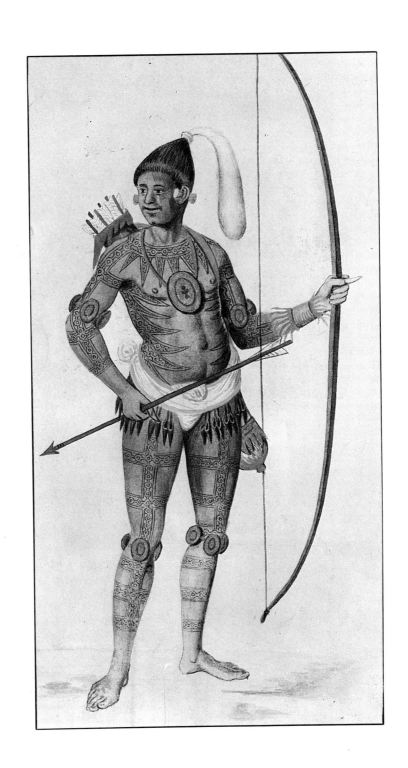

THE JUNIOR LIBRARY OF
AMERICAN INDIANS

THE SEMINOLE INDIANS

Philip Koslow

CHELSEA JUNIORS
a division of CHELSEA HOUSE PUBLISHERS

FRONTISPIECE: Chief of a Florida tribe, drawn by the English colonist John White around 1585.

CHAPTER TITLE ORNAMENT: Dolls in traditional Seminole women's dress have been popular souvenirs ever since tourists began flocking to Florida early in the 20th century.

English-language words that are italicized in the text can be found in the glossary at the back of the book.

Chelsea House Publishers

EDITORIAL DIRECTOR Richard Rennert
EXECUTIVE MANAGING EDITOR Karyn Gullen Browne
COPY CHIEF Robin James
PICTURE EDITOR Adrian G. Allen
ART DIRECTOR Robert Mitchell
MANUFACTURING DIRECTOR Gerald Levine
PRODUCTION COORDINATOR Marie Claire Cebrián-Ume

The Junior Library of American Indians

SENIOR EDITOR Ann-Jeanette Campbell

Staff for THE SEMINOLE INDIANS

EDITORIAL ASSISTANTS Annie McDonnell, Joy Sanchez
ASSISTANT DESIGNER John Infantino
PICTURE RESEARCHER Sandy Jones
COVER ILLUSTRATOR Hal Just

First Printing

1 3 5 7 9 8 6 4 2

Library of Congress Cataloging-in-Publication Data

Koslow, Philip.
The Seminole Indians / Philip Koslow.
  p. cm. — (The Junior library of American Indians)
Includes index.
ISBN 0-7910-1672-2.
      0-7910-2486-5 (pbk.)
1. Seminole Indians — Juvenile literature. [1. Seminole Indians. 2. Indians of North America.] I. Title. II. Series.
E99.S28K67 1994   93-35441
975.8'004973—dc20   CIP
                                                                AC

CONTENTS

The flat, swampy terrain
of the southernmost tip
of Florida, known as the
Everglades, became
home to the Seminoles.

CHAPTER 1

People of the Everglades

At the southernmost tip of the United States, bordering on Florida Bay and the Gulf of Mexico, there is a large tract of land called the Everglades. More than a million acres of swamp, forest, and prairie, the Everglades is home to a huge variety of plants, animals, and birds. The flat landscape is dotted with stately palm trees, tall cypresses thickly covered with drooping curtains of Spanish moss, and groves of mangroves whose clawlike roots form a barrier that no traveler can pass. In the shallow inlets, long-legged herons, ibises, and bitterns spear fish with their quick, sharp bills. Menacing alligators, ancient

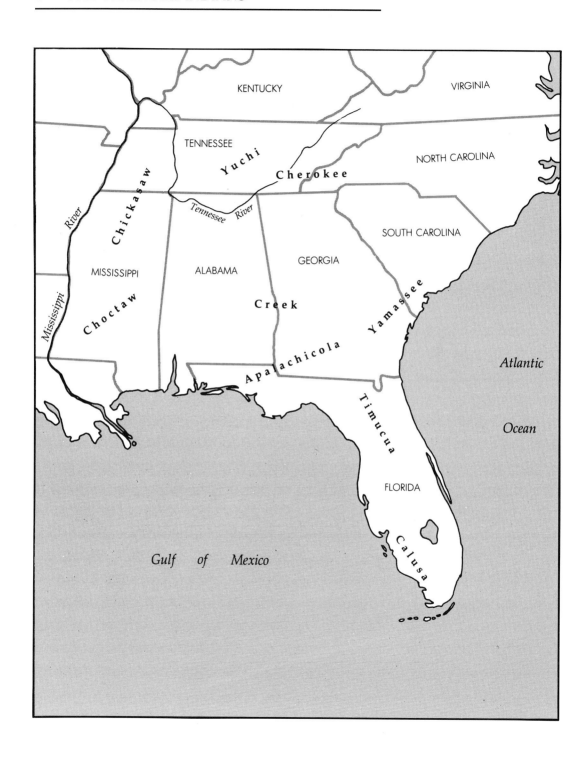

Several Indian tribes living separately in what is now the southeastern United States banded together in Florida to form one tribe— the Seminoles.

turtles, and gentle manatees navigate the rivers and the coastal waters. In the forests, mountain lions, deer, otters, and raccoons roam as freely as they did thousands of years ago. After nightfall, there is little to be heard except the *drone* of the insects and the hooting of the owls.

Today, all these creatures live under the protection of the U.S. government and the state of Florida. Since 1947, the Everglades has been a national park and wildlife preserve. But more than a century before that, the Everglades was the domain of a proud nation of people, one of the few Native-American tribes the U.S. government could never conquer—the Seminoles.

Early in their history, the people now known as the Seminoles belonged to a number of different tribes, including the Creeks, Choctaws, Chickasaws, Cherokees, Yuchis, Yamassees, Apalachicolas, Timucuas, and Calusas. Each tribe had its own language, history, customs, and myths. Some farmed, others hunted and gathered. For centuries, they lived in the present-day states of Georgia, Alabama, and Florida.

It cannot be said exactly when members of these different tribes came to be accepted as one tribe and called Seminoles. But as a result of natural migration and forced relocation, they made their way to Florida. There, they banded together, with each other and later with runaway black slaves. Over time, they became a unit. Just as the United States is a nation of peoples that came from different countries, so the Seminole tribe is made of peoples that came from different tribes.

Beginning in the late 1500s, Europeans came to the eastern shores of North America. As the newcomers increased, they cut down the forests and built cities, changing the world the Indians had known. By the late 1700s, there was a new nation on the continent, the United States of America.

As the nation grew and its citizens *clamored* for land, the government of the United States moved the Indians of the Southeast from their ancestral territory. The Seminoles refused to go. Thousands lost their lives in two bloody wars with the U.S. Army, and the survivors withdrew to the southernmost tip of Florida. The army could not fight the Seminoles in the tangled swamps, so the Indians were left alone to build a new life in the Everglades.

The Seminoles had to adapt quickly to the new environment. In their old homeland many of them had been farmers and cattle raisers, but the Everglades provided no grasslands for grazing and very poor soil for farming. The Indians managed to plant a few crops by building mounds on higher ground, but the thin soil was soon exhausted. In order to have enough food, the Seminoles learned to gather and cook wild plants. In addition, they caught fish and hunted the animals and birds that *abounded* in the Everglades.

In their former territory, the Seminoles had lived in large villages headed by male chiefs and less prominent tribal leaders. In the Everglades, the Seminoles organized themselves into small camps. This made it easier for them to find new places to plant crops and to follow the movements of the animals they hunted. By frequently changing location, they also made it harder for government troops to find and attack them. Non-Indians (then mostly hunters and outlaws) who ventured into the Everglades rarely saw a Seminole. These newcomers claimed, however, that as long as they were in the swamps, they felt that someone was watching every move they made.

Anyone who came upon a Seminole camp would have seen several rough buildings, known in the Seminole language as *chickees* (pronounced chick-EES). The chickees were made from the strong, straight trunks of the palmetto palms found in the Everglades. Be-

cause the weather was often hot and humid, the chickees were open on all four sides to admit cooling breezes. The Seminoles covered the roofs of their dwellings with the thick, fan-shaped fronds, or leaves, of the palmettos. They raised the floors of the chickees more than two feet above the ground, so that water and mud would not flow into the houses during the heavy rains of summer and early autumn.

Seminole families did not use only one dwelling for all their activities. Instead, they had a separate chickee for each part of their

The Seminoles called their traditional houses chickees. Raised above the ground and open on all four sides, they were suited to the warm and rainy Florida environment.

daily routine. They would use one building for cooking and eating, another for sleeping, and a third for relaxing and telling stories. It was easy for them to pack up and move to a new camp because they used no furniture: the Indians sat directly on the platforms of their houses and unrolled woven mats for sleeping.

By the time they established their new way of life in the Everglades, the Seminoles had suffered greatly. Thousands of them had been killed in warfare, and their tribal leadership had broken down. The ways of life they had known for centuries had been destroyed forever. And yet the Seminoles survived. In the safety of the swamps, they could gather in their palm-thatched chickees after the evening meal and tell stories of the terrible and glorious events that had made them the people of the Everglades. ▲

Indian men clad in
loincloths gather
wild rice, one of the
Seminoles' staple foods.

CHAPTER 2

The Old Southeast

In 1513, the Spanish explorer Juan Ponce de León set out from the island of Puerto Rico with three ships. He was searching for gold and also for a magical fountain that was supposed to make old people young again. He failed to find either the gold or the fountain of youth, but he did sight the shores of a land that was not on his maps. He named the land Florida, because of the many flowers (*flores* in Spanish) that he saw, and returned home without setting foot on it. Eight years later, Ponce de León returned and tried to set up a Spanish colony in Florida. The local Indians attacked the intruders and drove them off;

CORVERA

Explorer Juan Ponce de León was the first to claim Florida for Spain, although he had not yet set foot on it.

Ponce de León was wounded in the fight and died shortly afterward.

Other Spaniards followed Ponce de León, and Spain claimed Florida as part of its empire. Spain had established several colonies in the Americas since the first voyage of Christopher Columbus in 1492. The most important were Mexico and Peru, which provided vast amounts of gold and silver for the Spanish crown. The Spaniards failed to find any riches in Florida, however, and they soon lost interest in settling there. Instead, they built forts along the coast in order to protect their merchant ships from pirates and to keep other nations from setting up colonies. Their contact with the Indians was limited mostly to brief *skirmishes* when the Indians tried to prevent the Europeans from building their forts.

The land occupied by the Indians at this time was known for its lush forests and broad rivers. Most of the Indians lived in the river valleys, where the soil was rich and suitable for farming. When they farmed, the Indians grew maize (corn), beans, and squash. These crops were their basic foods, though they also fished, hunted, and gathered wild plants and herbs.

The Spaniards described the Indians of the Southeast as being tall, with olive-colored or brown skin; those who lived in the mountains were lighter skinned. The men wore leather loincloths around their midsections and sometimes leather leggings. Women wore leather skirts and shawls made of cloth woven from the bark of trees and other plant

The buildings here are not chickees, but the layout is typical of a Seminole village: surrounded by palisades, with the chief's house at center.

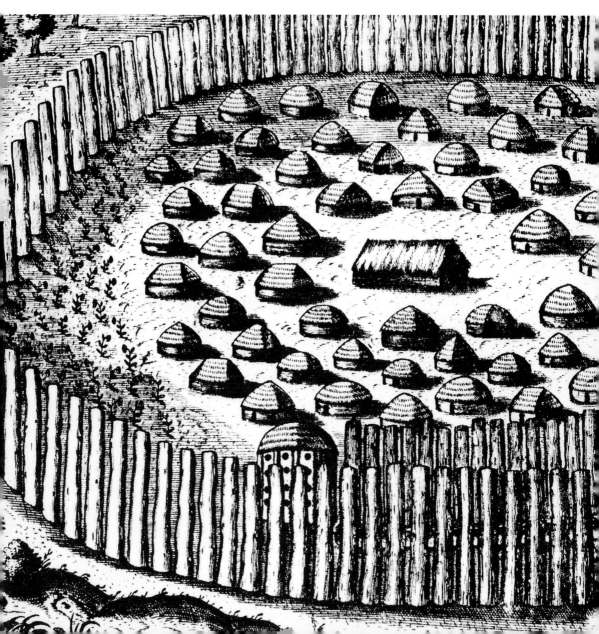

fibers. During the winter, both men and women wore robes made of bearskin or the fur of other animals.

The Indians of the Southeast used simple tools and weapons made of stone, animal bone, or wood. For hunting, the men used spears, bows and arrows, or blowguns with poison darts. They caught fish by making traps, or weirs, out of woven reeds, branches, or piles of rocks. Once the fish were trapped, the Indians often pulled them out of the water by hand. When they wanted to clear land for farming, the Indians would usually set fire to a section of the forest rather than cut down the trees. The crops were grown by the women, who turned the soil with pointed sticks. Before the arrival of the Europeans, the Indians had no knowledge of firearms or of iron tools and weapons. However, they were highly skilled at making canoes out of bark and carving dugouts from cypress logs. Some of the canoes were 40 or 50 feet long, and the Indians were said to travel in them as far as Cuba, 90 miles from the southern tip of Florida.

In the old Southeast, the Indians had lived in villages that were meant to be permanent. A village contained between 20 and 100 houses. The population of a village ranged from 100 to more than 1,000. Unlike the rough Seminole camps of later days, the villages were carefully planned. The house of the village chief was located at the center, along with a meeting house and buildings for storing food. The houses of individual families were sturdily built of tree trunks lashed together with reeds. Most families had summer and winter houses because the weather in central and northern Florida can turn quite chilly during the winter months. The winter houses were closed on all sides and often insulated with clay, whereas the summer houses were mostly open. Palisades, large fences made of logs, surrounded some of the villages.

The Indians of the Southeast spoke a number of different languages, and it was often impossible for groups to understand one another. Because they could not communicate, they could not organize themselves beyond their separate villages. Each village had its own life and made its own decisions. Sometimes villages formed loose *alliances*, holding ceremonies and celebrations together. But in times of hardship or war, there was no guarantee that the villages would help each other.

Within the villages, Indian society was organized into *clans*, groups based on descent from a common ancestor. Men and women usually married outside their own clan, and children always belonged to their mother's clan. Girls were taught by their mother to do the farming, weaving, and food preparation. Boys were taught hunting, fishing, and various crafts, not by their father but by one of their mother's brothers. Fathers were expected to provide for their children and to show affection for them, but because they were not members of the children's clan they did not play a dominant role in child rearing.

Warfare between villages was an important part of Indian life. The Indians fought in order to take prisoners, to get revenge on their enemies, or simply to gain glory. Young boys dreamed of making a name for themselves by returning from battle with the scalps of their enemies. Successful warriors were entitled to tattoo their bodies and wear eagle feathers; eventually, they would be given a place of honor on the village council. However, the Indians did not fight large-scale wars for the control of territory. This was a European idea, foreign to their way of life, but before long they would become all too familiar with it.

In 1565, when the Spaniards finally succeeded in building a settlement at St. Augustine, on the eastern coast of Florida, their control extended north to what is now the

state of Georgia. Contact between Indians and Europeans increased. In most cases, the Indians welcomed the Europeans. They were awed by the newcomers' ships, armor, and weapons, and were eager to have these powerful friends join them in war against their enemies.

Unfortunately for the Indians, the Europeans instead drew them into European war: the growing conflict between Spain and Great Britain. Great Britain had established its own colony farther north, in Virginia, and was battling Spain for supremacy in both Europe and the New World.

Those Indians who sided with the English were supplied with guns. The Spanish had

A map of Sir Francis Drake's attack on the Spanish settlement of St. Augustine in 1586. Drake's victory would have meant more territory claimed for England, but the British could not take the Spanish fortress.

always refused to arm their Indian allies. They were afraid that one day the Indians might turn those guns back on them. For this reason, some groups of Indians became stronger than others and were able to kill and capture their enemies in large numbers. The Europeans also brought many diseases the Indians had never had before, which caused the deaths of many natives.

As British forces gained more and more control of the Southeast, English settlers began moving into this territory, simply taking the Indians' land. Many Indians fled to Spanish-held territory in Florida, where they were often joined by escaped African slaves. The non-Europeans in Florida soon became known as Seminoles. The name was derived from a Creek Indian word, *simanoli*, which meant "runaway."

During the later 1700s, the Seminoles made peace with both the British and the Spanish. Their way of life improved as they began to raise crops such as melons and oranges, which the Spanish had introduced into the Americas. The Spanish also showed the Seminoles how to keep horses, cows, and pigs, and some Indians owned large herds of cattle. The old Southeast was destined to undergo many more changes, however, and the days of peace were not to last. ▲

*Seminole war chief
Osceola, who led the
tribe during the Second
Seminole War (1835–42).*

CHAPTER 3

The
Seminole Wars

In 1781, the American colonies won their independence from Great Britain. After the United States came into being in 1789, the new nation began to expand rapidly. As new settlers flocked to the Southeast, they pushed the Indians out of Georgia and Alabama and into northern Florida. Many of these new settlers were farmers who raised cotton and other crops and used slaves who had been brought to North America from Africa to work in the fields. When slaves escaped, they often crossed the border into Florida and lived with the Indians. Florida was still under the control of Spain, so the slaves and Indians felt safe there. However, land-hungry Americans were steadily pushing south, and they often engaged in skirmishes with the Indians. Both sides were guilty of savage acts.

In 1817, the United States declared war on the Seminoles, and the First Seminole War began. The government claimed that it was fighting the war in order to capture runaway slaves, but the government's true goal was to push the Spaniards out of Florida and open the territory to the American settlers. The U.S. troops that invaded Florida were led by Colonel Andrew Jackson, a tough, battle-hardened soldier known to his troops as Old Hickory. Jackson had the Indians outmanned and outgunned, but the Seminoles were determined to resist. Led by their chief Billy Bowlegs, they engaged Jackson's army in a fierce battle at Old Town, now known as Tallahassee. The Indians fought bravely, but they were no match for the well-trained and heavily armed soldiers. Those Seminoles who were not killed or captured retreated into the safety of the *marshes.*

The First Seminole War convinced the Spanish that they had no chance of holding on to Florida. In 1821, Spain officially sold Florida to the United States. The sale spelled doom for the Seminoles for although the

Colonel Andrew Jackson led the U.S. troops that invaded Florida in 1817. Jackson, who later became president, wanted to open up the territory to settlers.

Spaniards had often been cruel and greedy, they had looked upon the Seminoles and other Indian peoples as subjects of the Spanish king, just as they themselves were. They had tried to convert the Indians to Catholicism, and in many parts of the Americas, Spaniards and Indians had intermarried. The U.S. government, on the other hand, simply wanted the Indians out of the way.

In September 1823, 70 Seminole chiefs met with Governor William P. DuVal in St. Augustine. The chiefs agreed to move to a *reservation* in central Florida. In return, the U.S. government *recognized* the Seminoles as a separate Indian nation. The treaty that the Seminoles signed promised them farming equipment and cattle, protection from settlers, and a yearly payment of money.

When the Seminoles settled on their reservation, they discovered that they had made a poor bargain. The soil in central Florida was not good for farming. The area did not have the game and wild plants the Indians had found in their former lands. Before long, the Indians were going hungry. In spite of the treaty, non-Indians continued to raid the Seminole villages in search of runaway black slaves.

The capture of Seminole chiefs by U.S. troops during the First Seminole War (1817–18).

When the Seminoles' former land in northern Florida was all taken, the settlers began to demand more land. The U.S. Congress then passed the Indian Removal Act of 1830. Under this law, all the Indians in the East, including the Seminoles, were to be moved to a new territory west of the Mississippi River. The Seminoles had little hope of changing the government's decision. Their old enemy, Andrew "Old Hickory" Jackson, had become president of the United States, and he was determined to carry out the removal plan.

In 1832, seven Seminole chiefs traveled to the West to look over the proposed new home for the tribe. While they were there, some of them signed a treaty agreeing to the move. But the Seminoles had not given the chiefs the authority to do this. When the chiefs returned, they said that they had been tricked and pressured into signing the treaty. Hearing this, the Seminoles declared that they would not move to the West. The government insisted that the treaty was legal and told the Seminoles they would have to leave Florida by the year 1836.

Some of the Seminoles decided to obey the government's orders. Others decided to resist. In December 1835, defiant Seminole warriors made two attacks on U.S. troops based in Florida. This was the beginning of the Second Seminole War.

During the war, the Seminoles rallied around a proud warrior named Osceola. Osceola was one of the chiefs who had visited the West in 1832. Unlike some of his fellow

"The only treaty I will sign is with this!" said Osceola as he plunged his knife into the document that called for the removal of the Seminoles from Florida.

Seminoles, he had angrily refused to sign the treaty agreeing to removal. "The only treaty I will sign is with this!" he had declared, plunging his knife into the document as it lay on a table.

Because of his determination and his talents as a commander, Osceola became the Seminoles' leading war chief. He realized that the Indians could not defeat the army in open battle, and he taught his warriors how to conceal themselves in the wilderness and attack from ambush. In a message to the army, Osceola vowed that the Indians would continue to fight "until the last drop of the Seminole's blood has moistened the dust of his hunting grounds."

As the Second Seminole War raged on, 10,000 U.S. troops attacked the Seminoles in their villages. The soldiers destroyed the Indians' crops, scattered their livestock, and killed and captured many people. In the fall of 1837, the troops captured an important Seminole chief named King Philip. A group of 80 Seminole warriors, including Osceola, met with one of the U.S. commanders, General Joseph M. Hernandez, to ask for King Philip's release. Although the Indians had arrived at the meeting under a white flag of truce, Hernandez had them arrested and put in jail in St. Augustine.

Hernandez and his superior officer, General Thomas S. Jesup, congratulated themselves on their cleverness. Now that the Seminole leaders were in jail, they thought that the rest of the tribe would surrender. This did not happen.

continued on page 41

PATCHES OF COLOR

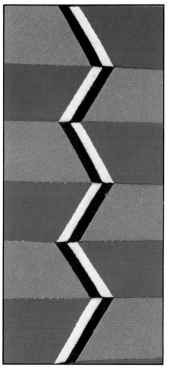

A close-up of a Seminole patchwork strip. Many small patches are stitched together to form a strip long enough to band a skirt.

The Seminoles obtained many new objects from non-Indian traders during the 1800s. At the end of the century, one of the objects the Seminoles acquired was the hand-cranked sewing machine, which soon changed their style of clothing.

Seminole women began to sew strips of brightly colored cloth onto traditional calico shirts and skirts. The stitches and decorations became more and more intricate as scraps of material in patchwork designs were pieced together and then were sewn onto pieces of clothing. Many patterns were named after the objects they suggested, such as a spool of thread or an arrow. Or a design was named after the woman who created it. These elaborate patterns were often copied, which was considered an honor for the designer. In gatherings much like the quilting bees of non-Indian women, Seminole women met to sew and chat, but each worked on her own sewing independent of the others.

The different reservations also had distinctive traditions. At Big Cypress, the women used six or seven smaller bands to decorate their clothing, while at Brighton the women used one wide band. Today, many Seminole women continue the tradition, creating and sewing colorful patterns and stitchery.

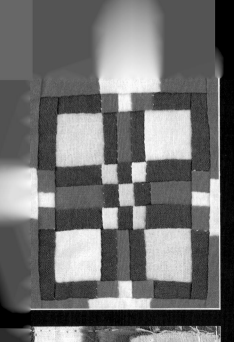

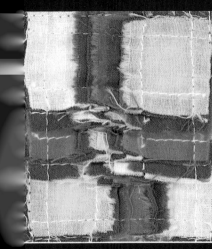

A patch in the checkers pattern resembles some variations of the traditional nine-patch used in American quilts. The wrong side of the patch shows how the cloth pieces are fitted and stitched together.

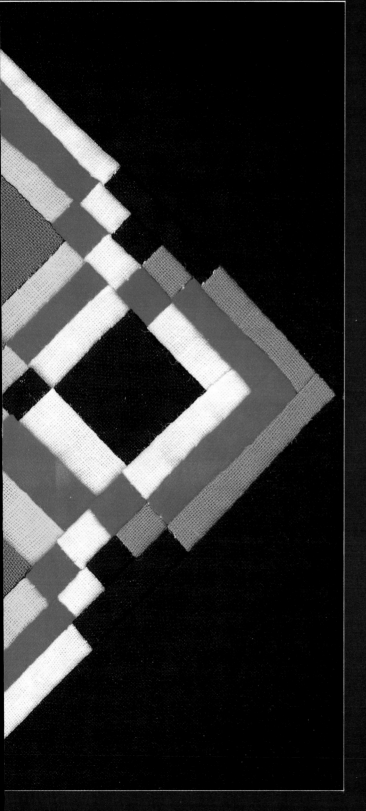

Some patchwork designs have been used by Seminole women on all the reservations for many years. Sewers often modify traditional patterns. At left is one variation of the checkers design.

The right and wrong sides of the patchwork design known as arrows.

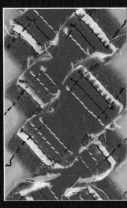

Traditional designs are often named for objects they resemble. This design, which looks like spools of thread leaning against one another, is known as spools.

A variation of the checkers design.

The creator of this design called it "flash" because it reminded her of the bolt of lightning emblazoned on the chest of the comic-strip character Flash.

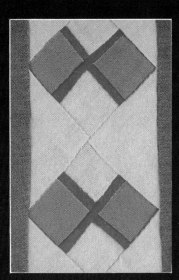

The right and wrong sides of a strip containing the design known as Xs.

A close-up of one patch in the rattlesnake design. A row of these patches sewn in a continuous strip resembles the diamondback rattler.

The right and wrong sides of a strip of patches in another version of the checkers pattern.

A man's shirt typical of the style worn by the Seminole in the early 1900s.

A woman's skirt and cape dating from the 1940s. The sewer combined thin bands of ribbon trim with wider strips of patchwork.

continued from page 32

While the war continued, the prisoners were patiently sawing through an iron bar that blocked an opening in the roof of the jail. After several weeks of work, some of the imprisoned Seminoles loosened the bar and made their escape, but Osceola was not among them. Afterward, he was moved to a more secure prison at Fort Moultrie in South Carolina. Early the next year he died there. Even though Osceola was an enemy, his exploits had won him the admiration of the U.S. soldiers. They buried him with full military honors outside the fort.

The government clearly hoped that the death of Osceola would crush the spirit of the Seminoles, but they were mistaken. The Seminoles fought on under a new leader, Cooacooche, also known as Wildcat. Wildcat, the son of King Philip, was one of the Seminoles who had escaped from jail in St. Augustine. He was determined to resist relocation to the West at any cost. "I would rather be killed by a white man in Florida than die in Arkansas," he declared.

By 1841, the Seminoles realized that the army simply had too many soldiers and too many weapons for them to resist. Most agreed to move to the West, but others

retreated to the Everglades, where the soldiers found it difficult to pursue them. Wildcat
himself remained in Florida until 1858, when
he finally surrendered to the army, saying,

Seminole warriors attack a U.S. military post during the Second Seminole War (1835–42).

"I am about to leave Florida forever and have done nothing to disgrace it. It was my home; I loved it, and to leave it is like burying my wife and child."

The Second Seminole War ended officially in 1842. The U.S. government had spent $20 million and had lost 1,500 soldiers trying to conquer the Seminoles, but it never got what it wanted. The Seminoles never officially signed the treaty agreeing to move westward—the treaty that the great Osceola had defiantly pierced with his knife. ▲

A typically dressed Seminole family in the 19th century. Before European influence, the Seminoles wore very little clothing at all.

CHAPTER 4

Changing Times

After the end of the Second Seminole War, the Seminoles who remained in Florida were left in peace for the rest of the 1800s. Many non-Indians were settling in the coastal towns of southern Florida, such as Miami and Fort Myers, but few of them wanted to brave the mysterious Everglades. The only non-Indians the Seminoles saw were the traders who sold them the goods they needed. In return, the traders bought feathers, otter hides, and alligator skins from the Indians. These items were very popular in the women's fashions of the day, especially the plumes of the white heron and the egret, which were used to decorate hats.

The Seminoles also hunted many animals for food, including deer, bear, raccoons, squirrels, and rabbits. In addition, they grew most of their own fruits and vegetables. But they had developed a taste for goods from the outside world. For example, they now hunted with rifles rather than spears or bows and arrows. Like non-Indians, they had begun to drink coffee and use tobacco. Because they now dressed in cloth rather than leather, they needed to acquire fabric from the outside world. They had also come to use U.S. currency in their business dealings.

In their manner of dress, the Seminoles were now quite different from the Indians who had greeted the first Europeans. The men wore loose cotton tunics that came down to the knees and were tied at the waist with a belt or sash. They also wore cotton turbans on their heads and cotton leggings. Women wore long skirts and covered their shoulders with colorful shawls. The women's dresses became even more striking during the later 1800s, when sewing machines came into use. The new machines allowed the Seminole women to sew complicated patchwork designs into their garments, a skill that has continued to the present day.

The Seminoles made great efforts during the peace of the mid-1800s to create tribal unity. Because their camps were so widely scattered, however, it was difficult to achieve this goal. Additionally, there was sometimes a language barrier between Seminole groups. The Seminole languages belonged to the *Muskhogean* language family. Within this family there were a number of individual languages. Some Seminoles spoke *Muskogee,* and others spoke *Mikasuki.* These languages are as different as English and German (which also belong to one language family), so Seminoles from different groups were often unable to understand each other.

Despite the difficulties the Seminoles faced, their physical isolation did bring safety. However, this too was bound to change. As the 1900s began, the United States was becoming a rich and powerful nation. People from all parts of the world came to live and work in America; as the population grew, more and more of the nation's wilderness was replaced by cultivated land, cities, and towns. Southern Florida, with its mild winters, had one of the fastest growing populations of any area in the country.

In 1905, the Florida *legislature* approved a plan to drain the Everglades. This project would provide fresh water for the settlements on the coast and make more land suitable for farming and building. At the same time, rail-roads were extending their tracks down the eastern seaboard, bringing more and more settlers to Florida. By the 1920s, Florida was one of the most popular vacation spots in the United States, with no end in sight to the build-ing of houses, hotels, and resort communities.

Acre by acre, the Seminoles' world was shrinking. In 1911, the Bureau of Indian Af-fairs (BIA), the U.S. government agency that regulates the nation's relations with Indian tribes, set up two reservations for the Semi-noles—the Big Cypress Reservation and the Dania Reservation. Big Cypress is located in central Florida, near Lake Okeechobee, and covers 42,800 acres. The Dania Reservation is located on the eastern coast of Florida, near Hollywood, now a popular vacation and retirement spot. Dania is much smaller than Big Cypress, but since 1926 it has been home to the BIA's Seminole agency. The agency carries out U.S. government policy regarding the tribe.

When the reservations were opened, some Seminoles moved onto them right away. Others, remembering the tribe's past exper-iences with the government, chose to try and preserve their old way of life in the isolated camps of the Everglades instead.

In 1921, this barge was used to drain swamps in the Everglades in an effort to create more usable land and to bring drinking water to the coastal cities.

The attitude of those staying off the reservation was expressed by a delegate to the Society of American Indians in 1911:

We have nothing to do with the United States government. This home belongs to us according to the treaties made with our ancestors. No white man south of the Chattahoochee River has any business here. This is our home and our land, and we will never leave it. We have a right to govern ourselves.

Whether they chose to move to the reservations or not, all Seminoles were being forced to adapt to a changing world. For example, at the turn of the century, the European clothing industry relied on imported animal hides—including alligator skins—and bird feathers for its fashions. A good part of the Seminoles' income had come from this trade. When World War I (1914–18) broke out, however, it was too difficult to get these goods from the United States and the styles of dress changed.

As a result of the decrease in trade, the Seminoles turned to other methods of earning money. They made dolls out of palmetto fibers and dressed them in Indian costumes. The dolls became popular with the many tourists who visited Florida. Seminole men also made money from the tourist trade by serving as guides for visiting hunters.

Now that Native Americans no longer stood in the way of settlement and development, they were viewed with interest and sympathy by many non-Indians. Before long, the Seminoles themselves became tourist attractions. Owners of resorts encouraged the Indians to come to non-Indian communities and set up their traditional chickees, allowing vacationers to observe their way of life. In some locations, Seminole men earned money by wrestling with alligators, a sport that made football seem tame by comparison. Many Seminoles enjoyed their contact

Florida became one of the most fashionable vacation spots in the United States in the early 20th century.

with the tourists and felt that they were well paid for their efforts. Others were suspicious of non-Indians or believed that such work was demeaning—without honor. They felt that the Seminoles should avoid non-Indians as much as possible.

When the *Great Depression* hit the United States in 1929, jobs were hard to find anywhere, and many Americans suffered great hardship. On the whole, the Seminoles may have been better equipped than others to deal with hard times, because they were used to living off the land. However, they still needed tools and other goods, and so they often hired themselves out as farm workers to earn some cash. In an effort to help the Indians financially and to encourage them to live on the reservations, the government created jobs clearing reservation land for farming. In 1935, a third reservation, the Brighton Reservation, was built at the northern end of Lake Okeechobee.

During the 1940s, more and more Seminoles moved onto the reservations. Though they continued to live in chickees, their lives had changed in other ways. Like most other Americans, they had discovered the automobile. While the Seminoles usually could not afford new cars, they learned auto mechanics so that they could keep their old, used vehicles running. Seminole children began to attend school, either on the reservations or in nearby communities, which was a major departure from tradition for the Seminoles. It wasn't until the 1940s that the first Seminole student earned a high school diploma.

The Seminoles had by now adapted to the non-Indian world. They had learned to make a living under difficult conditions and had become less suspicious of outsiders. But they still suffered from a lack of *unification* in their own community. Language barriers still existed, as Muskogee speakers lived on one reservation and Mikasuki speakers on another. Without tribal unity, it would be difficult to address and solve the problems shared by all the individual groups. Creating a political identity was the next challenge facing these resourceful people. ▲

The committee that wrote the constitution of the Seminole Tribe of Florida in 1957.

CHAPTER 5

Creating a Tribe

By the 1950s, almost all the Seminoles in Florida had come to live on the reservations. Only a small group held out. Most of these Seminoles lived along Route 41, a major highway that runs across southern Florida. This road had been cut through the Everglades during the 1920s, and it followed an old Indian path known as the Tamiami Trail. For this reason, the families who lived along Route 41 were known as the Tamiami Indians or Trail Indians. Unlike the rest of the Seminoles, the Tamiami Indians were determined to maintain their old way of life and avoid contact with the non-Indian world.

The Seminoles who lived on the reservations enjoyed many advantages, but they still suffered from a lack of leadership. They needed to speak with a single voice when dealing with the federal, state, and local governments. Finally, in 1957, the Seminoles took advantage of the *Indian Reorganization Act (IRA)*, a law passed by the U.S. Congress in 1934, which allowed them to elect their own officials. Under the IRA, the Seminoles were also able to draw up a *constitution* and to create a legal body known as the Seminole Tribe of Florida. This constitution is still in force today.

Under the 1957 constitution, the government of the Seminole Tribe of Florida is made up of two bodies: a council and a board of directors. Each of the three reservations elects one council member and one board member. Thus, the council and the board consist of three members each.

The job of the council is to communicate with outside government agencies and to enforce the laws of the tribe. The board of directors handles the tribe's business affairs and decides how to manage whatever money belongs to the tribe as a whole. Both the council and the board meet on the old Dania Reservation, now known as the Hollywood Reservation. This reservation has been the tribal headquarters since 1957.

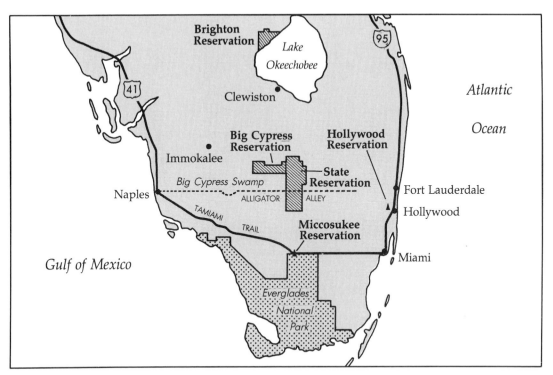

Locations of Seminole reservations in southern Florida.

All Indians who are at least one-quarter Seminole can belong to the Seminole Tribe of Florida. But only those Seminoles living on the Florida reservations can vote in elections for the tribal council and board of directors. For this reason, the Tamiami Indians set up their own government in 1962, calling themselves the Miccosukee tribe. The federal government granted the Miccosukees land for their tribal headquarters, and this is where most Miccosukees live. As this land is located on the northern border of the Everglades, some of them work as guides for

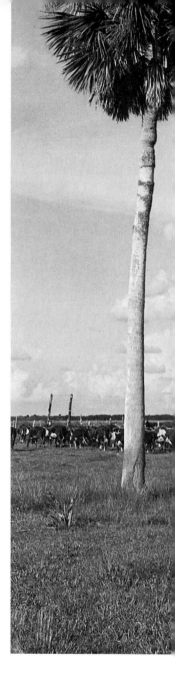

visitors to Everglades National Park. A number of Miccosukees continue to live elsewhere along the Tamiami Trail, squatting
(living illegally) in small camps, where they
hunt and fish and sell souvenirs to tourists.

Those Seminoles who moved to the West
after the Second Seminole War settled in
Oklahoma and continue to live there. However, they are not recognized as being part of
the Seminole tribe, and they have lost most
of their original Seminole customs.

The creation of a tribal organization was a
far-reaching event in the history of the Seminoles. For one thing, it gave the Indians a
renewed sense of pride and identity; now they
could shape their own future. One of the tribe's
first decisions was to make better use of the
land on the reservations. The Seminoles began
by *leasing* some of their tribal lands to
vegetable growers, who had to drain the land
in order to plant their crops on it. After a period
of years, when the growers returned the land,
what had once been swampland unsuitable
for crops was now fertile, rich farmland. It
had been transformed at no cost to the Seminoles. The tribe also made it a priority to build
better roads on its land, increasing members'
ability to get on and off the reservation.

When the vegetable growers returned the
improved lands, the Seminoles decided to

The Seminoles began raising cattle on the Big Cypress and Brighton reservations. The area's cattle industry remains prosperous today.

create pastures from them instead of farms, for the land was now able to support much higher quality grass for grazing than the native grasses found in Florida. Once the new grasses were established, the Seminoles were able to raise cattle on the Big Cypress

and Brighton reservations. The business was a financial success, and it gained respect for the Seminoles throughout the state.

During the late 1940s, the Seminoles gave up their traditional chickees for houses made of cement blocks. The cement block structures, or CBSs, were popular in Florida because of their sturdy construction. Unlike

Seminole women look over a cement block structure (CBS) in 1956. The CBSs, made to withstand hurricanes, were houses constructed by the U.S. government to replace Seminole chickees.

chickees, CBSs could survive the high winds of a hurricane, a constant threat in southern Florida. For this reason, the state urged the Seminoles to adopt this new style of dwelling. The CBSs were usually single-level houses consisting of three bedrooms, a living room, a kitchen, and a bathroom.

Moving from chickees into CBSs was a major change for the Seminoles. To begin with, different chickees had been built for different uses, such as sleeping, cooking and eating, and relaxing, but each CBS was intended for all uses. Previously, the Seminoles had slept on mats and sat directly on the floors of the chickees when eating or relaxing. Now the Seminoles had to get used to furniture. Instead of cooking over an open fire, Seminoles had to learn to cook on a stove and in an oven; instead of storing food in jars, they began to use refrigerators; and, rather than hunt their own food, they usually shopped for it in grocery stores. For the first time, the Seminoles would have indoor plumbing.

Understandably, not all Seminoles cared for the new housing. The CBSs were expensive to buy, and they were often uncomfortable. Summers in southern Florida are known for 90-degree temperatures and high humidity. The Seminoles' chickees had been open on all sides to let cooling breezes in, but the CBSs were completely *enclosed* and could become unbearably hot. By the mid-1960s, the Seminoles had worked out a plan with the state to build housing that would be sturdy and comfortable at the same time.

The new houses had all the modern conveniences of the CBSs, but in other respects they were similar to the chickees. Instead of a single large house, each family now had three smaller units grouped around a small courtyard: one for sleeping, one for cooking, and one housing a bathroom. The units were not enclosed like the CBSs but had large screened windows on all sides. The windows could be closed during the cooler weather and opened during the summer. The tribe and the state also worked out a plan that would make the new housing more affordable than the CBSs. The plan was to create self-help housing, meaning that the Seminoles themselves were expected to do some of the building, such as carpentry and painting, thus saving the expense of outside workers.

With new housing came new family patterns for the Seminoles. While in the camps, the Indians had lived in extended families, which included grandparents, aunts, uncles, cousins, and other relatives. Children in extended families were cared for by many different adults rather than just their parents. Now the Seminoles were more likely to form smaller family groups, similar to those of the non-Indian society around them. As the Seminoles had more contact with outsiders, they became more interested in the benefits of modern life, such as material goods and education, and they began to desire that modern life for their children.▲

A Seminole mother arranges her daughter's hair. Wearing this traditional hairstyle is one of many vanishing Seminole customs.

CHAPTER 6

The Seminoles Today

At the present time, the Seminoles' way of life is very similar to that of non-Indians. Some Seminoles run their own businesses, and some make money from crafts and handiwork. Many Seminoles work for fruit and vegetable growers. Others work for construction companies, building roads in the rapidly developing region of southern Florida. Seminoles who have learned to operate heavy road-building equipment earn high wages and respect.

The Seminoles' choice of jobs is often limited because the larger Big Cypress and

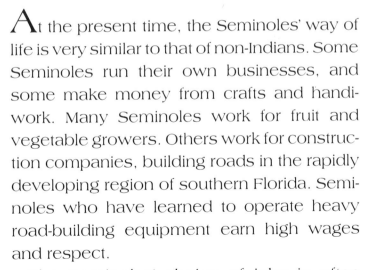

Brighton reservations are fairly distant from major cities. Often, when Seminoles work for large fruit and vegetable growers, they live in temporary housing at the job location and return home after the growing season. The Seminoles who live on the Hollywood Reservation have a much easier time finding jobs because Hollywood is a growing community and is near two major cities: Miami and Fort Lauderdale.

A number of Seminoles work for the Seminole Tribe of Florida, carrying out various duties. Others work for the federal agency

On the Hollywood Reservation, the souvenir shop and reconstructed Seminole village are tourist attractions that raise money for the tribe.

that manages the government's relations with the tribe. The Indian Village Enterprise, a re-created authentic Seminole village, is also a source of jobs for the tribespeople. Tourists pay a fee to visit the village and see how the Seminoles lived in years gone by. There visitors also can buy traditional Seminole handicrafts.

In the 1980s, the Seminole Tribe of Florida made the controversial decision to build bingo parlors on its reservations. Many individual Seminoles and non-Indians who disapproved of gambling opposed this decision, but the tribe believed it could earn a good income from the fees paid by the bingo players. The Seminoles constructed simple buildings large enough to hold thousands of people, and many gamblers now come by bus from distant communities, hoping to win big prizes playing bingo.

Even though they have changed in many ways, the Seminoles still preserve a number of their old traditions. Food is one of their main links to the past. For example, the Seminoles still drink *sofki*, which is made from mashed corn mixed with water. They also eat *frybread*, a food common to many other Indian tribes, which is basically a large fried biscuit made of wheat flour. Another favorite Seminole food is swamp cabbage, the buds of the sabal palmetto tree. Known elsewhere as hearts of palm, swamp cabbage tastes a little like celery and can be cooked in a number of ways or eaten raw. It grows plentifully on the reservations.

Some of the older Seminole women continue to wear traditional dresses of colorful strips and patches, topped by cotton shawls and many strings of beads. Older men may still wear the old-style cotton tunics that reach down to the knee. But most Seminoles began to dress like non-Indians during the 1960s.

Although the Seminoles no longer organize their communities around clans, the clan is still very important in Seminole life. Each Seminole still belongs to his or her mother's clan, and all Seminoles know which clan they belong to. People are still urged to marry outside their clan, but this custom is not as strong today as it was in the old days. Seminoles are not actively encouraged to marry non-Indians, but when it happens, the non-Indian husband or wife and the couple's children are fully accepted by the tribe.

Today, Seminole babies are born in the hospital like the majority of non-Indian babies. But many Seminoles still follow old traditions when their children are born. Little girls have their ears pierced as soon as they are brought home. (Once it was also customary to pierce the ears of little boys, but that is no longer general practice.) At the age of four months, both boys and girls have their hair cut and their fingernails clipped. The parents save the hair and nail clippings and give them to the children when they grow up.

In the past, babies were given one Indian name four days after birth. Now, however, because both a first and last name are required on state birth certificates, babies usually receive a non-Indian first name and their father's last name when they are born. (Some sounds in the Seminole languages cannot be written in the English alphabet, which is one reason why a non-Indian name is given on the birth certificate.) Many babies are still given Indian names during their first week, and these names will be used by their parents and other close relatives.

All Seminole children now attend school. The Big Cypress Reservation has its own elementary school, but children from the Hollywood and Brighton reservations attend off-reservation schools from the beginning of their education. It is now common for Seminoles to earn high school diplomas, and a number have gone on to college.

In the 1950s, Seminoles began in large numbers to adopt Christianity in place of their tribal religion. The old beliefs taught that the

Guests perform the Green Corn Dance after the wedding ceremony of Chief Tony Tommy and Edna John Osceola. The Green Corn Dance is a ceremony of purification, forgiveness, and thanksgiving. Such ceremonies are thought to keep the world in order by eliminating spiritual pollution.

world was full of many spirits and ghosts; that *inanimate* objects as well as certain people had magical powers; and that the sun and fire were special, important beings. Although some Seminoles have kept to their traditional religion, the reservations now have a number of Christian churches, and services are conducted both in English and in the Seminole languages. The tribe as a whole is very tolerant of different beliefs, and there is no conflict between non-Christians and Christians. In some cases, the Seminoles have blended the old beliefs with Christian teachings. For example, one Seminole story about the creation of the world begins with Fishakikomechi—not the Christian God—as the creator, but then goes on to tell about Adam and Eve, Noah's ark, and Jesus—all from the Christian Bible.

The Green Corn Dance is one of the most important traditional Seminole religious ceremonies. It is still performed from time to time, but some Seminoles believe it should cease because it is not performed or witnessed in the proper religious spirit. The tribe continues to host *powwows* regularly. Held in the summer at one of the reservations, the powwows are celebrations that bring all the Seminoles together for feasting, exhibitions,

crafts, and sports. The powwows attract a number of tourists and provide extra income for the tribe.

In general, the Seminoles who live on the Hollywood Reservation have adapted the most to non-Indian customs and ways of life. They have more contact with the larger society and more access to its jobs, education, and leisure activities. By contrast, the members of the Miccosukee tribe, those who

Billy Cypress being sworn in as the chairman of the Miccosukee Tribe of Indians.

still live along the Tamiami Trail, have maintained more of the old traditions. However they have chosen to live, all Seminoles share the pride of belonging to a people that has never lost its independence.

Any Seminole looking at a map of Florida will recognize many place names that derive from the Seminole languages. Tallahassee, Florida's capital, takes its name from a Muskogee word that means "old town." Lake Okeechobee means "big water" in the Mikasuki language. The Caloosahatchee River of the Everglades is named after the Calusa Indians, one of the tribes that came together to form the Seminoles. Osceola County pays tribute to the Seminoles' great war chief. Even more important, however, is the living presence of the Seminoles themselves, a tribe that has suffered much over the centuries but has truly never been defeated.▲

GLOSSARY

abound   to flourish or thrive

alliance   a pact or union between peoples or governments that promise to assist one another in times of trouble

chickee   the traditional housing of the Seminole, built with a raised platform for a floor and open sides in place of walls

clamor   loud noise or commotion; to protest or fight

clan   a group of families whose members share a common ancestor

constitution   a collection of basic principles and laws that determine the powers and responsibilities of a government and guarantee certain rights to the people it governs

drone   a constant low noise, such as buzzing

enclose   to surround on all sides

frybread   a fried biscuit, or bread, common in Native American diets

Great Depression   a time of severe poverty and unemployment in the United States and the world, beginning in 1929 and lasting through the 1930s

inanimate   not alive; without consciousness or spirit

Indian Reorganization Act (IRA)   a federal law passed in 1934 that allowed tribes of Indians to elect their own officials on their reservations and write their own constitutions

lease   an agreement to take possession of something for a period of time in exchange for some kind of payment

legislature	a group of people with the power to make and change laws
marsh	an area of wet land; swamp
powwow	an Indian social gathering with feasting, dancing, rituals, and crafts; now often held as a tourist attraction
recognize	to acknowledge the rightful existence of a nation's government
reservation	an area of land designated by the U.S. government, within which Indian tribes were forcibly settled
skirmish	a small battle or conflict
unification	the joining of individual groups to become one

CHRONOLOGY

1513 Juan Ponce de León sights uncharted land and names it Florida

1521 Ponce de León attempts to set up a Spanish colony in Florida; local Indians drive settlers off

1565 Spaniards build settlement in St. Augustine, Florida

1781 American colonies win independence from Great Britain

1789 The United States becomes a nation

1817 The United States declares war on the Seminoles—First Seminole War begins

1823 The United States recognizes the Seminole tribe as an Indian nation

1830 Indian Removal Act passed, allowing the relocation of Indian tribes to lands west of the Mississippi River

1832 Some Seminole chiefs sign a treaty to move to the West

1835–42 Second Seminole War with the United States

1837 U.S. troops capture Seminole chief King Philip; Osceola and 80 warriors are taken prisoner while negotiating his release

1905 Florida legislature approves plan to drain the Everglades

1911 The Big Cypress Reservation and the Dania Reservation are created for the Seminole

1935 The Brighton Reservation is built

1947 The Everglades is named as a national park and wildlife preserve

1957 The Seminoles draw up their own constitution and create a legal body—the Seminole Tribe of Florida

INDEX

ABOUT THE AUTHOR

PHILIP KOSLOW is a New York–based writer and editor with wide-ranging interests in history and literature. The editor of numerous volumes for young readers, he is also the author of *The Securities and Exchange Commission* in the Chelsea House KNOW YOUR GOVERNMENT series and *El Cid* in the HISPANICS OF ACHIEVEMENT series.

PICTURE CREDITS

　　我敢肯定地说，孩子、家长和老师们将会爱上这些画风亲切朴素，却能给孩子奠定做人标准的图书。这套图书是对儿童进行基础素质修养教育（如善解人意、相互尊重、协作以及友善待人等等）的有力工具，本套书表达直观、见解深刻，能帮助孩子们形象化地认识到：适当的行为举止可以积极地影响自我的发展及他人的态度，是实用、可信、权威、经典的儿童情商教育读本，我真诚地为孩子们推荐这套书。

——史蒂芬·柯维博士（《高效能人士的七个习惯》作者）

注意安全

[美]谢利·J·梅纳斯/文
[美]梅瑞狄斯·约翰逊/图
王伟男/编译

乐乐趣

未来出版社
Future Publishing House

图书在版编目（CIP）数据

注意安全 / （美）梅纳斯编文 ；（美）约翰逊绘 ；
荣信文化编译. -- 西安 ：未来出版社，2011.6
　（长大我最棒！）
　ISBN 978-7-5417-4298-9

Ⅰ．①注… Ⅱ．①梅… ②约… ③荣… Ⅲ．①能力培
养—学前教育—教学参考资料 Ⅳ．①G613

中国版本图书馆CIP数据核字（2011）第109194号

著作权合同登记号：陕版出图字25-2011-041
注意安全　Zhuyi Anquan
文字：[美]谢利·J·梅纳斯
绘图：[美]梅瑞狄斯·约翰逊
编译：王伟男
丛书策划：尹秉礼　陆三强　孙肇志
编辑顾问：袁秋香
丛书统筹：王元　张羽高　尹康琪
责任编辑：王元　高梅
特约编辑：张红艳
美术编辑：董晓明　金辉
技术监制：慕战军　段辉
发行总监：陈刚　雷彬礼
出版发行：未来出版社
出品策划：西安荣信文化产业发展有限公司
印刷：广东九州阳光传媒股份有限公司印务分公司
书号：ISBN 978-7-5417-4298-9
版次：2011年8月　第1版
印次：2012年2月　第3次
定价：180.00元（共15册）
网址：www.lelequ.com
联系电话：029-89189322

乐乐趣品牌归西安荣信文化
产业发展有限公司独家拥有
版权所有　翻印必究

献给每个阅读本书的孩子，
愿本书中的理念和爱你的
人们能帮助你注意安全。

致 谢

　　感谢梅瑞狄斯·约翰逊为本书配上迷人的插图，感谢玛里克·海莱因充满活力与热情的版面设计，感谢朱迪·加尔布雷斯等朋友们对这套书的热忱支持。我特别要感谢玛吉·利索夫斯基斯，这位经验老到、极富天分的编辑为本书增色不少。还要感谢哲学博士玛丽·简·韦斯在社会技能教育方面对本系列图书的指导。最后，我要感谢我了不起的家人们：大卫、卡拉、埃里卡、詹姆斯、丹尼尔、朱莉娅和安德里亚——他们每一个人都启迪了我。

wǒ yào yǒu ān quán yì shí
我要有安全意识。

wǒ zhèng xué xí zhe zài xǔ duō qíng xíng xià zhào gù zì jǐ
我正学习着在许多情形下照顾自己。

bǎo zhèng ān quán de fāng fǎ zhī yī
保证安全的方法之一,

就是听我所信任的大人的话，

并按照指示来做。

wǒ zuò shì shí zǐ xì kǎo lù   cāo zuò shí xiǎo xīn jǐn shèn
我做事时仔细考虑，操作时小心谨慎。

wǒ néng chá jué dào yǒu xiē dōng xi kě néng huì shāng hài wǒ
我能察觉到有些东西可能会伤害我。

zuò rèn hé shì zhī qián
做任何事之前，

wǒ huì xiān nòng qīng chǔ zhè yàng zuò shì fǒu ān quán
我会先弄清楚这样做是否安全。

wǒ yuǎn lí wēi xiǎn de dōng xi
我远离危险的东西。

děng zhǎng dà yì xiē wǒ zài qù xué zhe shǐ yòng mǒu xiē dōng xi
等长大一些，我再去学着使用某些东西。

和大人或小伙伴外出时，
我会和他们待在一起。

宠物用品

女装

rú guǒ wǒ men zǒu sàn le   wǒ huì bǎo chí zhèn dìng
如果我们走散了，我会保持镇定。
wǒ huì dāi zài yuán dì děng zhe bié ren lái zhǎo wǒ
我会待在原地等着别人来找我。

zǒng huì yǒu rén lái bāng wǒ de
总会有人来帮我的。

wǒ yě kě yǐ xiàng fù jìn de gōng zuò rén yuán xún qiú bāng zhù
我也可以向附近的工作人员寻求帮助。

tè shū de gōng zuò rén yuán tōng cháng dài zhe huī zhāng huò xiōng pái
特殊的工作人员通常戴着徽章或胸牌，
huò chuān zhe tè shū de zhì fú
或穿着特殊的制服。

xū yào de shí hou wǒ huì xiàng tā men qiú zhù

需要的时候，我会向他们求助。

fā shēng jǐn jí shì jiàn de shí hou
发生紧急事件的时候，
wǒ huì dǎ diàn huà qiú zhù
我会打电话求助。

wǒ xǐ huan jié shí xīn péng you
我喜欢结识新朋友，
dà duō shù rén dōu hěn yǒu hǎo
大多数人都很友好。

dàn shì   wǒ bú huì hé mò shēng rén shuō huà
但是，我不会和陌生人说话——
chú fēi yǒu zhí dé xìn rèn de dà ren péi zhe wǒ
除非有值得信任的大人陪着我。

如果我不认识某个人，

或是感觉那人不怀好意，

wǒ kě yǐ bù lǐ tā　bìng qiě lí kāi
我可以不理他，并且离开。

如果有人让我和他一起做
不安全或不正确的事情，

wǒ huì shuō bù　　rán hòu wǒ huì dào ān quán de dì fang

我会说"不"，然后我会到安全的地方，

tōng zhī wǒ xìn rèn de dà ren

通知我信任的大人。

yǒu shí hou huì yǒu chū hū yì liào de shì qing fā shēng
有时候会有出乎意料的事情发生。

我会提前计划并作好应急准备。

zhè yàng　　dāng jǐn jí shì jiàn fā shēng shí
这样，当紧急事件发生时，
wǒ zǒng néng zhǎo dào bì xū pǐn
我总能找到必需品，

shēn biān de rén men yě huì bāng zhù wǒ

身边的人们也会帮助我。

维护安全的方法很多，我还在不断地学习着。

Stay away from danger.
远离危险。

Ask for help.
寻求帮助。

Follow directions and use things carefully.
按照说明，小心使用。

Emergencies—have a plan!
应对紧急状况。

wéi hù zì shēn ān quán de tóng shí

维护自身安全的同时，

wǒ yě huì guān zhù zhōu wéi rén men de ān quán

我也会关注周围人们的安全。

zhè yǒu zhù yú wǒ hé dà jiā hé mù xiāng chǔ

这有助于我和大家和睦相处。

家长和老师必读——
让孩子们更深刻地理解本书传达的理念

当阅读每一页内容时，您可以询问孩子：

· 在这幅图里，发生了什么事情？

以下是一些您可以和孩子讨论的话题：

第 1~9 页

· 哪个人很小心？你是怎么知道的？谁需要注意安全？他要怎样做？

· 在学校里维护安全的方法有哪些？在家里呢？在其他地方呢？（讨论不同情形下的不同安全规则）

· 你知道怎样安全地使用特定工具吗？如果有些工具使用不当，会怎么样？

· 为什么遵守安全指示很重要？这样做有助于你维护自身安全吗？

· 有哪些事（或工具）是你小时候不能做（或不能用）的？还有哪些事（或工具）是你现在也不能做（或不能用）的？

第 10~17 页

· 你喜欢和大人去哪些地方？喜欢和小伙伴去哪些地方？为什么外出时大家应该待在一起？

· 你曾经迷路过吗？你当时是怎么做的？如果下次发生同样的事情，你会怎么处理呢？

· 和同行的人走散时，为什么你应该待在原地不动？怎样才能让别人更容易找到你？（孩子们应该待在容易被看到的地方，等待同行者来寻找自己；或寻求自己信赖的大人，比如工作人员的帮助。）

· 特殊的工作人员是指哪些人？他们在哪工作？你怎么才能认出他们？（例如穿制服的警官，信息台的工作人员，戴胸牌的售货员等等。）

· 如果你走丢了，身边又没有特殊的工作人员，你会向谁寻求帮助呢？（身边有小孩的妈妈或老奶奶会比其他人可靠。）

· 在学校里，如果你需要帮助，应该去找谁呢？在邻居家、在公园里、在图书馆或朋友家呢？

· 遇到紧急事件时应该拨打什么电话号码？你需要提供什么信息？（你所遇到的问题和你所在的地址。）

· 在什么情况下你会拨打当地的紧急电话？

第 18~23 页

· 为什么独自一人的时候你不应该和陌生人交谈？

· 当你和大人，比如父母或老师在一起时，又应该如何应对陌生人呢？（向孩子解释这是安全的情形，所以应该礼貌友好地去交流。）

· 在什么情况下，你可能不得不和陌生的大人交谈？（如果一个小孩子迷路或与家人走散了，他可能需要找社区帮手，比如警官、保安人员或商店售货员等交谈。）

· 什么时候你会和陌生的小朋友说话呢？

· 哪些是值得你信任的、可以保护你的大人？

注意：要让孩子们知道，当有危险或有异常状况发生时，他们应当告诉大人。例如：来历不明的人触摸穿泳衣的孩子；有人恐吓、伤害、威胁孩子；或者其他可能损害孩子安全的事等。告诉孩子们，家长和老师想知道是否有人恐吓或伤害他们。让孩子们把自己担心的事情告诉您，即使有人警告他们不要说，他们也应该把这些事告诉值得信任的大人。

第 24~27 页

· 在我们住的地方会发生什么紧急事件呢？（比如断电、火灾、地震或洪水等等。讨论最可能发生的状况，但注意不要对孩子灌输太多细节。）

· 你曾经经历过什么紧急事件吗？你当时在哪里？你做了什么？我们应该怎样为紧急事件提前作好准备？

第 28~31 页

· 为什么保护自己的安全很重要？注意安全是怎样帮助人们和睦相处的？（人们在没有危险的时候会一起开心地玩，他们知道在不同的情形下应该做什么，他们会学习新的东西，也会对别人表示尊重。）

留心防范儿童侵害者：相对于陌生人而言，孩子们可能更容易被他们所熟悉的人侵害。所以，您应当让孩子把所有令他们感到不适的状况全部告诉您。

尽管如此，最有可能对您的孩子造成侵害的还是陌生人。无论是在商场，在上学路上，还是在邻居家里，您都应当让孩子们知道，您不会让陌生人去接他们。儿童侵害者对孩子们惯用的伎俩包括求助、给小礼物、请吃东西，或假装发生紧急事件（如骗孩子说：你爸爸受伤了，让我来接你）等。孩子们不应该向陌生人透露个人信息。唯一例外的情况是迷路或和家人走散时，确保让孩子们知道，发生这种情况时，他们应该向什么人求助。

在孩子使用互联网时，请使用过滤软件。将电脑放在家里或教室的开阔区域，当孩子上网的时候，请您尽量保证陪在孩子身边。切勿让孩子在互联网上透露个人信息（姓名、电话号码、家庭地址或自己的照片等）。叮嘱孩子在看到任何令他们不适的内容或信息时及时向您报告。

您应当经常和孩子或学生们阅读这本书。当孩子们熟悉了书的内容后，您就可以尝试在"教学契机"（美国心理学家布罗菲提出的认知心理学术语，指未经事先计划而出现的、学习者非常愿意学习新知识的时刻。也译为"可教时刻""可教育时机"等）出现时，将本书中涉及"注意安全"的理念传达给孩子们。当孩子在日常行为中表现出遵守安全准则、谨慎使用物品、回避危险场所或合理寻求帮助的行为时，您应当加以留心并给予表扬。此外，您还可以通过第34～35页的活动来强化孩子们对于注意安全的重要性的认识。

"安全"游戏

《注意安全》教孩子们学习关于个人安全最基本的信息。书中所提到的安全技能，按照其英文首字母，可缩略为英文单词SAFE（意为"安全"）。SAFE:S代表远离危险；A代表寻求帮助；F代表按照说明，小心使用；E代表应对紧急状况。

安全和危险（巩固"远离危险"技能）

材料：磁性白板、马克笔、磁铁片、杂志、卡片、剪刀、胶水。

准备：从杂志上剪下有不同的日常生活用品的图片，用胶水把它们粘在卡片上来制成一副卡组。在白板的左上角写"安全"，右上角写"危险"。

阶段1：将卡组面向下放置。请一个孩子抽出一张。提问："这幅图里发生了什么事情？这是安全的还是危险的？"或者"这样做会有人受到伤害吗？"然后让孩子依据自己的判断用磁铁片把卡片固定在"安全"或"危险"栏里。

阶段2：拿出分在"安全"栏的卡片，向孩子们提问："你怎样安全地使用这件物品？"让孩子说出或以角色扮演的方式表演出正确的使用方法。接着拿出"危险"栏中的卡片，向孩子们提问："如何避免在使用这些器具时受到伤害？"让孩子们把适当的应对方法（比如寻求帮助或远离危险等）以角色扮演的方式表演出来。

家庭和学校安全（巩固"远离危险""寻求帮助""按照说明，小心使用"的安全技能）

材料：颜色鲜艳的不干胶、小标签、马克笔。

准备：把小标签分为三组，在第一组上写"No"或者画一个大"X"（表示"远离危险"）；在第二组上画一幅大人和小孩的简笔画（表示"寻求帮助"）；在第三组上画一个笑脸（表示"按照说明，小心使用"）。

说明：和孩子讨论在学校或家庭中使用各种物品的潜在危险（例如风扇、电动工具、切纸机、加热器、插座、电线、熨斗、吹风机、卷发棒、火炉、汽油桶、烤架、剃须刀、洗衣机、药品等）。您应当强调大多数物品虽然都有重要用途，但是为了安全起见，必须小心地使用。看看屋子里哪些物品可能会给孩子带来潜在危险，帮助孩子分类：哪些是可以按照说明独自小心使用的，哪些需要在大人的帮助下使用，哪些应该远离。让孩子把不同的标签贴在相应的物品上。

"如果我走失了"角色扮演（巩固"寻求帮助""应对紧急状况"技能）

说明：讨论特殊的工作人员和他们的工作。问孩子："如果你在_____走失了，你应该怎么做？你应该向谁求助？"讨论孩子可能遇到的问题和他们应该求助的人。您可以参照第32页中针对本书第10~17页的内容提出的问题。

角色扮演：利用玩偶等道具让孩子表演在不同场景中走失的情景；让孩子针对该情况采取适当的行动，例如：将父母或监护人的名字告诉相关人员，必要时说出家庭住址、电话号码等。下面是场景和可以寻求的帮助者示例：

- 商场：售货员、收银员、信息台人员、保安
- 图书馆：管理员
- 海滩：救生员
- 服装店：店员
- 杂货店：收银员、负责人
- 公园或广场：带小孩的妈妈
- 电影院、剧院：检票员
- 学校：老师、校长
- 社区：认识的大人、警察

延伸讨论：与孩子讨论在不同环境中应对不同突发状况的策略。

朋友和陌生人（巩固"远离危险"的技能）

材料：杂志、卡片、剪刀、胶水、马克笔。

准备：从杂志上剪一些图片，用它们分别代表家人、朋友、孩子、特殊的工作人员、陌生人。（孩子们也可以自愿提供自己或家人的照片。）将图片粘在卡片上，然后正面朝下叠放起来。在两张空白的卡片上分别标上"朋友"和"陌生人"。

说明：单独和每个孩子来做游戏。从一叠卡片中翻过一张，提问："周围没有其他人的时候，你可以和这个人谈话吗？"孩子也许会回答："可以，这个人是我的家人（朋友或特殊的工作人员）。"或者"不可以，我不认识他（她）。"讨论过后，让孩子们把图片归类到"朋友"或"陌生人"组里。

延伸游戏：在不同情境下进行安全常识角色扮演。情境示例：单独去开门或接电话时；有陌生人询问、送礼物或让你搭便车时；看见某人需要帮助时；被大孩子欺负时；对某人（陌生人或熟悉的人）的言行觉得反感时；等等。

应对紧急情况（巩固"应对紧急状况"技能）

与孩子讨论可能会发生的紧急情况，以及应当采取的应对措施。针对下列情况，讨论应当采取的安全措施：遭遇火灾时；遭遇水灾时；待在结冰的湖面或河面上时；在公共汽车上时；骑自行车时；步行时；遭遇危险事物时；遇到陌生人时；遇到灾难撤离时；等等。询问孩子们："如果发生这些意外状况时，你会怎么办？"帮助孩子们想出答案，然后进行角色扮演。让孩子们对所在区域可能发生的紧急事件有所准备。在几天或数周后，以其他应急措施为主题，继续对孩子展开训练。

"长大我最棒！" 儿童健康心理与完美人格塑造图画书

礼貌和友善

如果孩子表现得有礼貌、尊重别人、态度友好，那他和别人的相处就会更加愉快。本书教孩子学会基本的礼貌和友善行为。

诚实和坦率

孩子可以学着选择说出事实，尽管那可能很难。本书教孩子保持诚实这种非常重要的品质，坦率行事，并勇于承担责任。

倾听和学习

倾听是一种重要的学习方法和沟通技巧。本书介绍了倾听的作用和具体方法，并将重点放在倾听所带来的正面效果上。

帮助和给予

就算是年纪很小的孩子，也能通过自己的一份努力而让世界变得更美好。本书教孩子慷慨行事、帮助他人、关怀社会。

尝试和坚持

勇于尝试、敢于坚持是通往成功的必备品质。本书鼓励孩子积极调整心态、坚持不懈地完成生活中的目标。

接纳和认同他人

世界正变得越来越多元化，这也体现在孩子的日常生活中。本书教孩子学会尊重不同，寻求相似，大度包容，欣赏他人本色等。

冷静和平息怒气

愤怒是一种负面的情绪。本书教孩子理性地认识愤怒，并提供各种有效的策略来帮助孩子建设性地应对自己的怒气。

懂得和遵守规则

不懂得遵守规则的孩子往往会陷入麻烦之中。本书教孩子懂得日常生活中最基本、最重要的规则。

爱护和管理物品

每样物品都有它应有的位置，如果爱护和照管得当，物品的寿命就可以更长久。本书教孩子学习照管物品，并了解关于尊重、责任、管理的知识。

加入和一起玩耍

结识新朋友，和大家一起玩耍，这是很有趣的事情。本书教孩子学习关于合作与相处、结识新朋友等方面的基本技能。

沟通和解决问题

孩子的生活中也会出现各种各样的问题，学会和平地解决冲突非常重要。本书教孩子学习沟通和解决问题的基本技能。

理解和关爱他人

善解人意是一种体验他人情绪和感觉的重要能力。本书教孩子学习理解他人的感受，聆听他人心声，懂得尊重他人。

克服恐惧

孩子在生活中会面临各种各样的恐惧，有真实的，也有臆想的。本书帮助孩子理解自己的恐惧，并学会克服恐惧的基本技巧。

学会分享

分享是一种重要的社会行为。本书教孩子学会与人合作及分享的各种基本方式：分发、共同使用、交换以及轮流等。

注意安全

对孩子来说，世界充满了危险。本书教孩子学习最基本、最重要的安全技能，学会保护自己和别人。